Beauty Fed My Poetic Soul

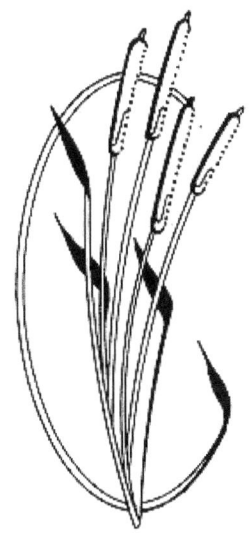

Beauty Fed My Poetic Soul

by
Dorothea Sharon

Editor & Proofreader
Emily Carte

Graphic Design by
Rashard Sharon

Senior Publisher
Steven Lawrence Hill Sr.

Awarded Publishing House
ASA Publishing Company
Established Since 2005

A Publisher Trademark Copy Page

ASA Publishing Company
Awarded Best Publisher for Quality Books 2008, 2009
Nominated for the Better Business Bureau 2012 Torch Award
105 E. Front St., Suite 201A, Monroe, Michigan 48161
United States of America
www.asapublishingcompany.com

All Rights Reserved. No part of this publication may be reproduced, stored in a retrieval system or transmitted in any form or by any means electronic, mechanical, photocopying, recording, taping, web distribution, information storage, or otherwise, without the prior written permission of the publisher. Author/writer rights to "Freedom of Speech" protected by and with the "1st Amendment" of the Constitution of the United States of America. This poetry is a work of fiction with non-fiction attributes and has a poetic dialect, spoken in a profession that can be used for educational and historical learning purposes. With this title page, the reader is notified that this text is an educational tool in poetic form, and the publisher does not assume, and expressly disclaims any obligation to obtain and/or include any other information other than that provided by the author. Any belief system, promotional motivations, including but not limited to the use of non-fiction characters and/or characteristics of this book, are within the boundaries of the author's own creativity and/or testimony in order to reflect the nature and concept of the book.

Any and all vending sales and distribution not permitted without full book cover and this title page.

Copyrights©2012 Dorothea Sharon, All Rights Reserved
Book: Beauty Fed My Poetic Soul
Date Published: 10.18.2012
Edition: 1 *Trade Paperback*
Book ASAPCID: 2380596
ISBN: 978-1-886528-41-3
Library of Congress Cataloging-in-Publication Data

This book was published in the United States of America.
State of Michigan

A Publisher Trademark Title page

In Memory

of

Bertha Sharon

George Sharon II

and

Mollie Belk

Table of Contents

Letter of Appreciation .... (a)

Preface .... (I)

Prayer .... (V)

Introduction .... (IX)

About the Author 91

O'Linda Boyd

The Beauty of Making It Happen 1

Dorothy Carter

The Beauty of a Grandmother's Love 5

Bertha Sharon

The Beauty of Building a Bridge 9

Charlotte Sharon

The Beauty of a Blended Family 13

Mollie Belk

The Beauty of a Neighborhood Love 17

Jeannie Communings

The Beauty of One Question 23

First Lady, Elder Sheila Vann

The Beauty of Dreaming 27

Mrs. Frances Small

The Beauty of Mothering Others 33

Mrs. Bernice Smith

The Beauty of Tradition 37

Alyson Williams

The Beauty of an Angel 41

Stephanie Hart

The Beauty of a Butterfly 45

Netfa-Enzinga

The Beauty of Freedom 51

Meagan Mitchell

The Beauty of Honesty 55

Dedicated to my Entire Family

The Beauty of Family 59

Dedicated to my Mothers, Sistas and Daughters

She Is 63

Dedicated to the Women of Second Ebenezer Church

The Beauty of Our Elders 67

This is dedicated to Lorraine, Beverly, Kori, Phyllis, Marvie, Tanisa, Keisha E., LaCrecia C., Wanda, Edrina, Shani, Tabitha and Lakeisha

The Beauty of My Sisters 71

Dedicated To Every Beautiful Woman

There's Something Wrong with Your Love Story 75

Inspired by Mary Henderson

Mary, Mary, the Hair Fairy 77

Inspired by Dr. Rebecca James Williams

The Beauty of Listening 79

Inspired by Ms. Patty

A Remodeled Angel 81

Inspired by the Documentary Love is Not a Black Eye

Love Is Not a Black Eye 83

Soul Sista #Won

The Beauty of My Sistas 87

(d)

Letter

of

Appreciation

    I thank God for His mercy and grace on this project. I owe God me because of how he so eloquently orchestrated this project with another divine daughter of Christ, Dr. Dana Teamor. I have come to experience God in a new way and I give him glory for His divine intervention and connection with Dr. Teamor. Kelly Wilson, thank you for all your assistance and diligence on this journey. My publisher Steven Hill, thank you for educating me on the process and moving this project expeditiously. You are a dream fairy for writers. Thank you for understanding it all. I'm blessed to have my project in your hands. My editor, Emily Carte, your patience and care on this project is priceless.

    There is no way that I could have completed this journey without the help and push from so many people. The loving support from my family in all my creative endeavors is one of the strongest reasons that I fight so hard to produce work that will make you all proud. I fight because I've seen your fights and have heard the fights of my elders; therefore I am determined to be a change agent that will lift and celebrate all mankind.

Dad, I did not become a black belt, but I did learn how to fight with my words. All of the karate, acting and dance classes helped me diversify my way of thinking and appreciate the differences of others. My family's presence and influence in my life is worthy of a standing ovation.

To my Mother, O'Linda Boyd, nothing beats a mother's love. Thank you for encouraging me to be the best at "whatever" I wanted to be. To my Dad, George Sharon, your "comeback fight" deserves an encore. You are my heavyweight champion. To my grandparents, Samp and Dorothy Carter, you are the reason I still believe in "black love." Charlotte Sharon, you've shown me how blessed I am to have two moms. To my siblings, Lorraine Kress, Otis Williams and Rashad Sharon, dreams are in our reach. I pray that all my nieces and nephews will read my work and model this quote, *"Let no one ever come to you without leaving better."* -Mother Teresa

To my loving church family, Second Ebenezer Church, thank you for all the support and affirmation you have blessed me with since the age of 12. Your support kept me encouraged and believing. Bishop Edgar L. Vann II and Elder First Lady Sheila Vann, thank you for your relentless teachings. Your teachings encourage me to keep God first in my gift with every project. Thank you both for sacrificing your youth so that others could pay it forward.

Derek Denham, thank you for all your support and all the brainstorming sessions. There is still more to come. Scott Allen Davis, the endless support you give provides strength and courage in my endeavors.

To the dream team of D.R.E.A.M. (Diamonds, Rubies, Emeralds *and* Me) Girls mentoring program, (Jor'Dawn and Stacie) I love serving with you all because your commitment shines for the girls that need us. We have real work to do. My experience with D.R.E.A.M. Girls helped me understand a greater need to publish this book; mentoring is not optional, it's necessary to connect in order to help build someone else's village.

I want to personally thank my brother, my friend, Ameir Hakeem for being a trailblazing poet. Your crazy moments at the mic inspire me to go higher. Khary and Tunesia Turner, my favorite couple in life, thank you for the years of singing, dreaming and performing on Rivard Street (memories for life). Marvie Wright, you are a great inspiration to me. You are my sister from another mother. We've got more stories to tell.

Thank you Jessica Care Moore, Debrena Jackson Gandy, Lorraine Hansberry, Nztoke Shange, Sista Souljah, Maya Angelo, Bell Hooks and many other women that are unafraid to put the truth to pages. You have inspired me to use my ink to reach the masses and ignite change. I thank God for our weapons of writing to help us with our wars.

To all my friends that called to check on me during this project. Thank you for the push, the pat on the back to keep me going (Kori, Tanisia, Wendy). Duane Davis, the best writing partner that anyone could be blessed to call a brother and a friend. Angela Barrow- Dunlap, thank you for my opportunity as a playwright. Thank you for showing me there is nothing too big for God. Evangelist Elaine Wright, your prayers have been truly a guiding light. Duane Davis, Angela Barrow-Dunlap, Marvie Wright, Keith and Mehmuna Jackson, Joe Smith, Alonzo Marable, Michael Brown and Gerald McBride, I thank God for our creative journey and experiences that helped me get to this place. Pioneering is our purpose.

To the entire Detroit poetry community, never stop because your words carry movement.

PREFACE

It is my sincere hope and prayer that every eye that reads this book will be compelled to grab hold to another woman, young girl and an elder to help flower their garden.

Turning forty was a momentous moment for me. It did not feel like any other birthday. I remember sitting down at a coffee shop and feeling the moment of where I was spiritually, financially, professionally and personally in life. I can recall revisiting some regrets, and also some celebrated and fulfilling times. Needless to say, I truly believe you do not make it to see forty without understanding that there were people that helped you make it that far.

Taking a close examination of myself, I realized that the woman I was twenty years ago is not the woman that I am today. My life experiences have enhanced my growth and development. However, I would be foolish to think that I could possibly take the credit for that. I have so many people, in particular women, who took their time, talent, resources and love to help cultivate my growth and development. I am so grateful to have had them in my life to plant seeds that would someday grow into my beautiful garden. Some of them planted seeds, some watered the garden, and so many of them brought sunshine. It is their selfless contributions that made the world of a difference in the choices I made and the roads that I have traveled.

I wanted this book to be reflective of the gratitude that I have for them. I am so grateful and blessed that there were women in my life that took my hand and guided me on a straight and narrow path when I was too young, too inexperienced to know otherwise. I am also grateful for those women that saw themselves in me and could see the road ahead and mistakes that could be avoided. They forewarned me of paths unknown. I am ever so grateful for those women that just set examples by their living and their lifestyles, demonstrating what it means to be lady and a woman of God. I am grateful for the women that saw something inside of me that was forbidden to lay dormant.

So, these women pushed, coached and encouraged me to go deep to find my passion and purpose. I consider these women to be my mentors, teachers, mothers, sisters and friends. Their giving and sacrifices made the difference in my world and who I am today. I will forever thank God for them and pray continuously that He awards favor in every assignment in their lives. These women mentioned in the following chapters have compelled me to write this book. My soul purpose is to encourage other women and young girls to give of themselves in ways that will make a positive impact in someone else's life.

Prayer

Dear God,

I pray that every woman and young girl who reads this book will be compelled to find the space and the love to reach back, reach out and reach up to be a help to another woman or girl. Even without knowing one another's story, allow us to identify a need and meet it.

Father God, allow us to become unafraid to share our stories with transparency to shield other women from the same pitfalls of life. Allow us to use our maternal instincts, godly wisdom, intuition and intellectual capacities to reform, reinvent and reaffirm one another. Give us the courage to pray for one another and petition you God on one another's behalf. Allow us to celebrate one another's successes. Help us to learn how to be a help for any bad bounces in life. Help us to continue to align our lifestyle according to Your will in order that we may model the behaviors of exemplary women of God.

Let us commit to being accountable and responsible in lending healthy and productive teachings and advice to other women that trust us. Help us to share more of our testimonies without the fear of judgment or retribution in order that we may help another woman along her journey. Let us never give up on one another inspite of our heartaches and hang-ups.

It is my desire that these pages of inspiration ignite a fire in our souls so high that it will move us to a place where women identify the need and the purpose to connect with each other. Regardless of our socioeconomic, cultural, ethnic, political and religious differences we can still lend value in each other's lives. In any case of where we have come from, where we are going, and where we live today, there is always hope that our garden can grow and blossom with the help of God and others to foster nourishment and growth.

Let us commit to help raise up a nation of women that will have pride, dignity, self respect and courage to do what is right, stand for what is right, and fight for what is right. We have to fight so that we do not leave it to popular culture to set the standards and expectations of what it means to be a woman. God, allow your light to shine in the face of many that will encounter our stories, wisdom, failures and successes in order that they understand what it means not only to be a woman, but a Godly woman.

I pray that every man and boy that chooses this book as a gift to another woman or girl will be blessed beyond measure. I pray that spiritual nourishment and growth will bud in your life and for your family as a result of you planting a seed in some woman's garden. I pray that it meet a vacant need in your family's life. I pray that they see these writings as an inspirational ride to build self esteem and or affirm their purpose. I hope that every reader is inspired and receives an internal push that forces them to do more to help and be a blessing in the lives of others.

(VIII)

INTRODUCTION

<u>Beauty Fed My Poetic Soul</u> features poetry that celebrates the women in my life that were instrumental in my development. Each poem is titled after that woman. This is my tribute to them. You will hear the myriad of ways they touched and impacted my life. There is a compilation section that I have included - these writings were birthed out of personal and intimate conversations that I've had with other women. These conversations, and in some cases, observations, left an imprint in my heart and stirred up my poetic voice; allowing me to express these findings and feelings.

As a young girl I can recall on many occasions listening to my grandmother's stories about life in the South. There was always mention about what they could and could not do "back then." Her stories provoked discussions of the morals and values of women of her times. I also understood how some traditions of the family and women were non-negotiable. Her stories, which always started with *"In my day..."* were the reflections of her days and times as a young woman. These discussions caused her to question what our day now looks like as women. Sadly, so many have strayed away from critical values and morals that historically preserved the moral fabric of women in their most desolate times. Based on my grandmother's recollections, moral integrity stood on the shoulders of gender relationships. In high esteem, she spoke of her grandmother, Moy, whom she dearly respected and loved. Her comedic illustrations of Moy would have you assuming she was Harriet Tubman! My great, great grandmother, Moy, whom I did enjoy as a young child during the last few years of her life, had high expectations for her children and set those standards in her household and teachings. The remnants of her teachings are still shared and passed along in my family today.

Just as my grandmother shared her stories of the women that shaped her life, I was inspired to do exactly same with my literary work of poetry. I was compelled to use my poetic voice to illustrate the importance of having women in your life who love and care about you. It is my desire that this book will penetrate the need to dismantle the complexities of gender disparities that lace together strands of resistance. We can no longer afford to proliferate and perpetuate stupendous perceptions and interactions with each other any longer. This type of gender segregation is dangerous to us, our families and our communities.

If we are unable to dialogue and relate to one another, then we have just dismantled the village that we know is needed to raise our sons and daughters. We must regain the cohesiveness and cooperative communities that will help guide our young people and groom them to live whole and healthy lives. The implications of remaining unaltered will cost us our children.

Ladies, we must fight against the occupying powers of jealousy, envy, gossip, toxic talks and judgments, low self-esteem, and many other ill behaviors that will continue to stall the blooming and bonding with each other. We need each other to raise our children and raise ourselves, to our highest potential in which God is calling us.

(XII)

Beauty Fed My Poetic Soul

by
Dorothea Sharon

"The Beauty of Making It Happen"

The Ojays, "It's a Family Reunion" - "Sadie...don't you know we love you sweet..." - The Spinners, Walter Hawkins and the Hawkins Family
I could never forget Tramaine Hawkins, singing "Be Grateful..."
These were the anthems that played in my household as early as I can remember.

Then I remember asking my momma for two afro puffs and a fuss it was between the comb and my hair
She mastered a way to do it, although she had a rough time getting my part real straight
Somehow she made it happen.

Sunny Delight Orange Juice, cheese toast, roast beef cooked in a crock pot and jiffy mix cornbread
Repeat young days when life rested on tradition, dinner conversations, setting the table and eating together
Giving of her younger years to be and become a mother.

Aborting, I'm sure, some of the plans she had for herself when she became a mother.

A fighter, a warrior and a woman all at the same time best describe who she is
She is the poster child for strength and my billboard of inspiration of the known phrase practiced daily, "Make it happen".

Her mental and emotional toughness sustained her to deal with stressful and painful situations through many of her tests and trials in life
Without ever losing faith she made it to the next page of her story
I began to understand the beauty of, "Making it happen".

My mother's strength is reminiscent of a super hero with super human powers, always making it happen.

Make it happen even if all the resources are not accounted for because God has gifted us all with talents that He said would make room for us.

Make it happen even if the only one believing, praying and seeking is you.

Activate that mustard seed of faith, and watch how things evolve and move.

Make it happen, inspite of the "naysayers"
Keep pushing, praying and pressing - nothing prospers from stressing
Just confess God's word: *"If you abide in me, and my words abide in you, you shall ask what you will, and it shall be done to you."*

My mother taught me that you don't have to let things happen when you are God's child
You have the power to make things happen
Speak, confess, voice, state, articulate and affirm your preferred future in Christ Jesus.

Thank you Ma, for the confirmed lessons in your living.

Dorothy

"THE BEAUTY OF A GRANDMOTHER'S LOVE"

Without Dorothy Carter, life could have seemed so much harder
But her prayers to God only grew louder
When life seemed uncertain at times, a prayer in her bosom she'd find.

She was always inclined to speak her mind
Speak to God with tears in her eyes with a "Yes, Lord" in her cries
And I'm certain she had a few "whys" in her eyes.

God, raise my family
God, guide me
God, give me the strength to keep on keeping on
God, help me to stay strong
God, please shine your face upon me to help me see that You have more in store for me
God, don't leave me alone
I trust that You will help me weather the storm
God, I trust that You will bless my home.

A song from her heart I would hear her sing
Lyrically ministering to a young girl's soulful dreams.

I'd hear, King Jesus, and My Savior, Precious Lord, and Great Almighty, then there would be Father God in Heaven
And I knew then the way she would wail out - that God loved us so much that He'd reach high and open up the skies for us.

Her life taught me how to be strong
No matter what lie in the wilderness
Don't allow bitterness or anything else to prevent me from passing life's tests and trials.

Her conversations with God were
Yes Lord, I've been tested and tried, but never once did I die
A stronger woman kept coming
Her faith in God kept growing
Strong winds kept blowing
But it never stood in the way of hymns she moaned that would change the mood.

A hot plate of eggs and grits and a sanctified prayer spoken over our food
Summer barbecues - front porch corn rolling - hot combs to those kitchen curls
Grabbing my neck so the comb wouldn't burn

She'd pop your hand with a feather comb, and tell you, "Move your hand, girl! I am down to my last curl."

Ooh - whee, I believe there was an awning out on the front porch that read, "Mrs. Carter's Hot Curls for Little Girls House of Beauty."

She is life, soul, a heart precious as gold
A storyteller
Her wise words she can still share over a hot plate of grits
Her Mississippi stories, her prayers, her laughter, her soul will forever be my strength to stay strong
Grow stronger
Keep my promise to God and give Him my very best
'cause Dorothy Carter, didn't raise no failures.

A woman who used her sanctified soul and soul stirring stories to show me that if you live long enough rough days may come
But with God, trouble will soon run.

Funny how small talks and intimate times over a bowl of grits can teach a young girl that with God, there will never be a need to quit.

Bertha

"THE BEAUTY OF BUILDING A BRIDGE"

Sewing machines, needles, colored threads, fabrics and patterns of materials was Grandma Bertha's house.

Childhood memories of a woman that took pride in fashion, and believed in living life like it was golden.

Her travels, I believe was her past time joy
Where she once dreamed, imagined and created her next adventure in life.

Visits with her felt like holidays
Always, because she was proud to be your Grandmother
The whole neighborhood knew it.

Niagara Falls, a memory that would forever impart itself on my life.

A still photo resides in my heart from an early childhood memory of a bus trip with Grandma
Holding my hand as we watched the water leap into what appeared as an endless pit
At that moment, I could feel what was assigned in her heart.

As we snuggled and struggled to stay warm against the fighting wet winds by the Falls

I looked in her eyes and felt her instructions:
Live life, travel, explore, take off the limits and be!
There is no harm in living as long as you're learning along your journey
Pass it on, pass it along
Hold on to the hand of each and every family member regardless of what is and what is not
Continue to build a bridge with love to bring someone else over.

Celebrate the smallest and the darndest of things with laughter, family and good times
Show up, dress up and if necessary make up
But wake up and remember you have a essential role
Keep your family together.

Her love as a seamstress gave her the working experience and the knowledge to adjust and alter straps, hems, add buttons, and add whatever finishing touches that she felt would beautify the garment.

Remove any wrinkles from the fabric to provide a fresh clean appearance

Preserve the garment in order to keep it safe and protected for years to come

She was the seamstress that kept the family together

Her gift gave her the ability to build a bridge that is still growing.

Thank you Grandma Bertha, for giving me the needle to keep sewing.

Charlotte

"THE BEAUTY OF A BLENDED FAMILY"

The last name, "Sharon" for this lady simply means shar-ing

Bright, shiny smiles and warm hugs have met me at the door for all of my life

"Love you, Baby," are the words that I hear at the beginning of every phone call and at the end of every goodbye.

Charlotte Sharon is not shy with her love
She lends solace and affirmation
Giving of herself is an illustration of God's love
You never leave her presence without feeling better.

Advice on how to get it together
Keep it together, and love forever are inspirations of her guided instructions on life and living
She is a giver
Giving of herself to help others succeed.

I am her daughter from another mother
But the love for her family (extended and all) doesn't stop at her biological children.

Her spiritual lending, giving and wisdom is the enchanted beauty of what keeps a blended family together.

Love for my Father God, and my father George, opened up the space to love his children
Just like the wind that breathes on the earth, the grass that clothes the dirt - Charlotte's love is one of the most astonishing gifts that bless the earth.

Her expression of love is the quintessential embodiment of a blended family.

Without any hesitations and reserved uncertainties
She accepts you for who you are and loves you where you are
And makes you a part of her family.

She brings the complete and absolute ingredient to a blended family...unconditional LOVE.

"The Beauty of a Neighborhood Love"

Street parties for kids on the blocks

"Hey, Mrs. Belk!" - "Hello, Mrs. Belk!" - I heard to and from my school walks.

The neighborhood knew her
The love in her smile came through her
Wherever she traveled
To the corner store, the beauty shop, the shopping center, the grocery store, and even school
Mrs. Belk was known, loved and respected in her neighborhood.

Five kids of her own,
Young, old, too grown, too smart to be told,
Never stopped her from loving you with that smile.

Walking the halls of Tendler Elementary School
Didn't matter to her if kids were cruel
Love still ruled
She never stopped loving you with her smile.

To the Lycaste block, and the entire neighborhood
She was more than Mrs. Belk doing whatever she could.

She was a nurse
A caretaker
A school teacher
A counselor
A tear wiper
The Neighborhood Watch
A cook
An aunt
A grandmother
A nurturer
A lover
A mother

Sweet potato pies, so sweet that it could wipe your weeping eyes. Fresh brewed ice tea made you fall on your knees
And ask God for forgiveness with a "please"!

Chicken salad with Miracle Whip Sandwich Spread
And even sometimes Peanut butter and jelly on a piece of toasted buttered bread.
The heart that packaged itself around a neighborhood.

Those that may have been pushed and shoved aside found a place to run and hide
In the hugs of a mother, an aunt, a neighbor, a teacher, a leader.

The heart that never denied love to all
An ability to clothe you with her God
Made you feel esteemed inspite of broken and brittle dreams.

Kool-Aid kids ran to her house for meals, and a cup of grape Kool-Aid
Receiving so much more that left their gentle souls full, happy and fed.

A people magnet she truly was
I truly believe it was love wrapped in all those hugs.

Aunt Mollie, your very beautiful gentle spirit will remain a momentous landscape that will prevent me from derailing my ability to love, removing all barriers and differences of others to make the space and the room to love.
Only the heart of a woman like Auntie Mollie could leave this pivotal teaching etched and scribed on the walls of my heart

"As long as you make space to love, you will always have the room to forgive."

-Inspired *by* Auntie Mollie

Jeannie

"THE BEAUTY OF ONE QUESTION"

She asked, "What do you want to be when you grow up?"
A simplistic question was asked, but a big answer was to accompany this.

A cousin with enough love for her little cousin
Planted the seed of
"What if."

What if I could become a professional actress?
I'd enroll in a performing arts school or college
take dance, piano and acting
I'd become a triple threat! Yep! That's what I'll do.
Then, I'd go on auditions, find an agent to get me work
And Ta-dah, I'd become the world greatest actress of all times.

There I am, at the Oscars reciting my acceptance speech
Long, flowy, sequined gown
Smiling at cameras and waving to fans
Eloquently with poise, stepping out of a limousine
Smiling, shaking hands and exchanging Hollywood hugs
Ah, that's what I want to be, all that and some.

She'd asked "what do you want to be when you grow up?'

Because she saw that life was bigger than my front porch.

She asked because she understood that I needed to see that there was more in store than what was just in front of me
She asked because she wanted me to start dreaming
So I could start thinking, planning, plotting on how to get there

Anywhere

Just go

Dream

Believe

And Become

Wow, one question can change the ride of your life.

First Lady Elder Sheila Vann
"THE BEAUTY OF DREAMING"

A heart enflamed and a soul enchanted with Love
A flower in a garden with beautiful folded petals
She's more than a photograph or a portrait, but a collage of God's possibilities.

Her words are light to the pathways of life
Wisdom flows from her heart and falls on ours.

She is far more than what you see
She gives birth to new ideas, dreams, new visions and new realities.

She is a Queen
A Queen that taught a young girl like me how to dream
And other young girls like me that trouble ain't all what it seem, when God is in the midst of things.

Replace my thoughts of "ice style" with a brand new life style
Holiness
Teaching that there is no loneliness, when God is holding us.

And…we must walk like a Queen and only a King will follow
She teaches us that we are priceless and not shallow.

She has helped so many women understand that we must love ourselves, respect ourselves and
Honor ourselves
Because we are made in the image and likeness of God.

Because First Lady, took the time to teach so many of us and labored just to reach us
Choices don't have to be so hard.

So thank you First Lady, your Dream Girl now knows and understands that
We must live
No more incarcerated dreams, no more awe… mercy…mercy…mercy things ain't what they use to be…naw… Its living life like it's golden, because I am a chosen generation, a royal priesthood, a holy nation.

We must laugh
Dance with the autumn leaves
Allow our faces to feel the cool breeze of old man winter
Smile at the sun in the summer
And watch a rose grow from cracks in the concrete in the spring.

See because laughter warms the heart, soothes the soul to all, young and old

It's a bold statement to God when he sees a frown upside down,

It's our response to him that says I love how you turn things around.

We must love without reservations, hesitation, stipulations, contemplation, promises of elevation.

Like the butterfly we must spread our wings and fly and believe that love is the wind beneath our wings

Love is the reason that we sing.

As a young girl destined to reach her dreams, I was encouraged to

Rise

Excel

Achieve

And Magnify God

A heart enflamed and a soul enchanted with Love

A flower in a garden with beautiful folded petals-

You're more than a photograph or a portrait, but a collage of God's possibilities.

Her words are light to the pathways of life
Wisdom flows from her heart and falls on ours.

She has helped me and many others believe
She gives birth to new ideas, dreams, new visions and new realities.

She is truly a Queen
Thank you, First Lady for helping me Dream.

Dorothea Sharon | 33

Mrs. Frances Small

"THE BEAUTY OF MOTHERING OTHERS"

Pineapple Sundaes, on Sunday, always
Benediction, church chicken, in the basement,
Fellowship with the saints
Auntie Pam's pound cake, mouth-watering dessert.

Next it was a walk down Cadillac Street
For a Sunday treat, before the 3:30 afternoon program.

Every Sunday, not only were the doors of Second Ebenezer Baptist Church open, but so was an invitation to Momma Small's house
Mrs. Small's house was open to five young girls – all from the church – Bambi, Beverly, Boo, Kathy and Kori (her daughter).

This was a ritual,
We hung together like it was spiritual, committal, literal

Walks to 3500 Cadillac was indeed our Sunday ritual,
See there was nothing small about Mrs. Frances Small
Five silly girls, she listened to Bubble Yum bubble gum,
Popping pop corn and sleepovers of giggling, laughing and crackin jokes,

But at the end of the day she had the patience and she gave of her time to make sure we heard sound advice
Didn't matter if we were naughty or nice, she told us what was right.

A burgundy Regal, was our ride to church musicals, church concerts, to school, the mall, the movies and anywhere else we wanted to go
She wasn't slow about taking us, and she wasn't slow about straightening us
If something wasn't right, she told us the truth to pour out some light.

Giving of herself for five silly young girls, meant the world to us
We know and understand that she had an invested interest to hear of us laugh,
To see us grow,
To see us enjoy life,
Get away from all the strife at home,
But most importantly,
We didn't have to be alone.

Five young girls, could have become "Girls from the Hood,"

But instead Mrs. Small understood,

That life can still be beautiful, dreams are still reachable,

And she made life teachable for five young girls

Still chewing bubble gum

She made life FUN!

Mrs. Bernice Smith

"THE BEAUTY OF TRADITION"

A warm fuzzy feeling
The aroma of a southern meal cooking
Bookcases beautified by pictures of the entire family, trophies and awards.

Every pillow, rug, placemat, centerpiece, and plant had a perfect place and space that it occupied
And the smell of homemade cookies.

Girls giggling on the front porch
Relay races in the street
Every neighbor said hello
There were no strangers to meet
Everyone knew everyone on the entire block.

And everyone knew Mrs. Smith's house.

She believed in adorning her house with sweetness, neatness, and tradition at its best
A mirror image of who she really was.

Beauty, unquestionable illumination of the warmth, calmness and competence of femininity

A satisfying aroma that adds pleasantry to the atmosphere.

She showed us the power of femininity
The purpose and influence of tradition
And we soon learned that some things shouldn't change
Like being a lady and keeping order in your home
Where things should be kept sacred, valued, appreciated and remain
She gave a "woman's touch" a face and a meaning
Compassion, patience, order, detail, grace.

Mrs. Smith preserved tradition as her womanly weapon
And made manners matter to us.

I reconnect, remember and I am reminded that beauty can be discovered in the smallest corners of tradition
Like Love in the smell of a fresh pot of boiling collard greens.

Mrs. Smith helped young girls like me understand what tradition really means.

"The Beauty of an Angel"

The first voice of Def Jam Records
She took her timeless voice and big heart to many stages and places around the world to give of herself.

Her songs danced with your heart, the unexplained magic she gave in every lyric sung was in concert with your emotions.

With music like hers, love could never go wrong.

Resurrecting days of production tours, planes, theater venues and dressing rooms
Alyson always made room to show others how much she cared about them.

From Jodeci concerts to the stage of the Apollo, and many theaters in between, was a big sister assigned to me
Alyson - "Alley".

Taking me under her wings to share with me things that could be done
Should be done, and ought not to be entertained
Will always resonate with me

Jewels of wisdom she shared with me.

Genuine love and concern for a younger sista, who's trying to understand how to survive and remain stabilized
In a world of entertainment.

Dressing room jokes, small talks, exchanges of hopes
How to climb the success ropes without choking
Her wings guided me along the way
A road she clearly traveled before, she used to guide me
In some instances hide me
From the cold storms of the unknown and things that were foreign to me.

Her wings helped me dream big enough
Her wings helped me learn I was good enough
Her wings, made me want to push hard enough
Her wings, made me want to sing loud enough
Thank God for the wings of an angel who cared enough
Her love and protection ushered me to fly while having the support of an angel's wing.

Stephanie

"THE BEAUTY OF A BUTTERFLY"

My girl

My friend

Many miles separated us

But our soul ties never left us.

No matter how long the days had past

It felt like yesterday when we saw each other last

Touring days of stage plays, dressing room jokes, prayer on tour buses.

We were sisters and we both understood that God brought us together to be there for one another.

There were days of Crenshaw Swap Meets, spa pedicures for the feet

Lynwood, Los Angeles, Melrose, Beverly Hills (Larry Parker's), Wilshire Boulevard, and we can never forget "The Alley".

Days of girlfriend talks

Shopping bags in hand

Making life plans and sharing our Hollywood dreams

Two girls that shared the exact favorite loves, God first and then shoes
We would always say that "All God's children need shoes"
We would say that all we wanted when we saw God in heaven was a new pair of shoes.

We watched each other grow in so many ways
That the best and brightest days is what we expected for one another.

We were each other's dream fairy
If there was a way to wave our magic wand we would manifest every requested dream it seemed.

Miles apart did not stop a sisterhood from growing
A true friendship that would glow as a flagship for what it means to be there through the best and hardest places in life
Being there to talk each other through
Being there to petition God for you
We were there.

We were there
Didn't matter what time the phone rung

A three hour time difference.

It was our sister duty and our "sister keeper" spirit and fight to listen and share what's right.

I made it to Los Angles on quick flight
But by then you had fought a good fight
God's plan arrived to take you home, my dearest girlfriend.

Oh, we had the best of times
From concerts, book signings, Momma Luci retreats, Larry Parker's to eat, pedicures, then new shoes for the feet,
Jewelry, make-up, hair, industry talks and long walks on Melrose Street, will be missed, but never forgotten
Because I will always repeat these memories.

My girl Steph,
I understand that your destination had to change
Your love and laughter will always remain.

You laughed and loved until time took your breath
God transitioned your life
But we still have your light

I will forever let your love live

Stephanie Hart

My girl

My friend

This is not the end, but God's transition to another place.

Love your Sister,

That saw the wings of a beautiful butterfly that wore the baddest pumps you've ever seen.

#

"THE BEAUTY OF FREEDOM"

Chile, stand up straight and project!

You got to feel from deep down!

You got to believe that "Thang!"

You have the power to take audiences anywhere you want them to go.

Netfa Enzinga,

Big personality, Big Voice, Big Talent

The stage is her opportunity to train, coach, educate and move many to an empowering and emancipating place of Freedom,

Freedom to Act

Freedom to Sing

Freedom to Create

Freedom to Scream

Freedom to Love

Freedom to Cry

Freedom to Feel

Freedom to Relive

Freedom to Reinvent

Freedom to Dance

Freedom to Recite

Freedom to Emulate

Freedom to Impersonate

Freedom to be Queen Sheba,

Freedom to be Hurt

Freedom to be…

One of my most influential acting teacher, and mentor

Empowered me with

Freedom to be

Without any apologies.

Thank you Netfa Enzinga, a fighter and a survivor of life.

"THE BEAUTY OF HONESTY"

A tall walk

Nothing short about her smile, her style, and heart full of glee
Kind of girl where her pinky finger stands alone whenever she's sipping on herbal tea, slowly.

But surely thinking, planning, designing and orchestrating her next business moves
Smooth, not to anxious to display knee jerking reactions.

Fractions of her creative flair, can easily be spotted on walls, patterns, fabrics, mixed media art, and whimsical décor to adorn her beauty institute - @ Meagan's.

Someone that transforms life's simplest pleasures into an amazing experience
That's the added value she brings with her to every conversation, service and even when you frequent her beauty institute.

Her conversations are beyond what she's putting on your hair, but rather,
"What are you putting in your head?"

She provokes thoughts, intentions, not to mention what's healthy and what's not, without any fear of judgment
You are free to be you.

You can be transparent and transformed at the same time in one conversation
She opens that door of time and opportunity for you with a warm smile, a loving touch and honesty that means so much.

It takes a tall woman to do a big thing and that is
practice honesty with integrity.

It's all in her style in how she's helping groom the world.

-Dedicated to my entire family-

"THE BEAUTY OF FAMILY"

A mother stands in the mirror with her daughter, as she dresses her with pearls of wisdom
Reflections of her younger self, she sees while she's passing words that have fallen on her ears from her mother that now spill from her lips *"You are fearfully and wonderfully made. Yes, you are precious."*

A father ties the laces of his son's shoes
While bended on one knee, he locks eyes with his son and make's the declaration, *"The steps of a good man are ordered by God. Remember, your steps are ordered."*

Family, the importance of it is so misunderstood
It is shades of mocha fingers snappin at family reunions and barbecues.

Its big hats, church fans, riding on church vans together and worshipping at the same church.

It's Pookie Man, Man-Man, Faye, and Lenroy in Grandma's kitchen, uncovering a boiling pot of mustards and turnips greens.

Sneaking a taste of Auntie Mollie's pinto beans
Watching Aunt Shirley perform her magic with a black iron skillet, whipping up hot water cornbread
It's the entire family sitting down, holding hands, bowed heads, prayin, and sharing this family's spread.

Cousin Cheryl's baby girl, single parent, two kids and nowhere to live
But the family loved her, supported her and prayed for her
Introduced her to the right man
She now understands how God will give you another chance.

Its little Tommy, who the hood thought wouldn't amount to anything
There the family stood on the bleachers
Cheered him on as he received his Doctorate's degree.

He now announces to those same folks that with God, you can do anything.

Family, it's laughing at Uncle Reggie's jokes, even when they aren't funny
Still praying, lifting and encouraging your cousin, who jumps out of an Escalade, spinner rims, music blaring and wearing a belt buckle that reads, "G- Money".

And yes it is loving your family behind penitentiary bars
Family embraces you with your mistakes, weakness and still loves you
It is through hang ups, break ups, make ups, and back together again, family.

A caro-soul ride of welcome and unwelcomed experiences, but it is still family
For better or worse
For richer or poorer
Through sickness and health
Family, tenderness, forgiveness, sweetness, weakness, through madness, sadness
It is all that.

Family is what keeps us praying, singing, rejoicing, and believing that God is still performing miracles.

-Dedicated to my Mothers, Sistas and Daughters-

"She Is"
"THE BEAUTY OF BEING REAL"

Full lips, wide hips, shades of darkness, kinky hair

No apologies for my uniqueness

My design was divine with revelational purpose assigned

See, I come from a long line of finger snappin, foot tappin, hand clappin, God praisin and hand raisin women, that understood that God was all she needed, whenever her soul started bleeding

Or her flesh needed feeding

It was God that did the pleasing.

Then there was, "Thank you Jesus," for making the way out of no way

Moving in my favor inspite of me standing in the way,

And they taught me how to sing

Wade in de water, God is going to trouble the waters
God's going to give me double for my trouble
And hey, trouble don't last always
God can give you strength to speak to the mountains and they be removed.

We come from powerful women who knew their strength
Who didn't just hold down a church bench, but trusted God every inch of their journey
And with every page of their story
Because they understood that their life and their light was to give God glory
Their proclamation is "Greater is He that is in me, than He that is in the world."

She is,
a worshipper, praiser, nurturer, encourager, courages, a "go-getter", dream maker, a mother, a sister, an aunt, a god mother, a good girlfriend, a best friend, as she holds on to God's unchanging hands.

If I am an expression of her, then my light and my life is on fire, for Christ.

I am she and she is Me.

-Dedicated to the Women of Second Ebenezer Church-

"THE BEAUTY OF OUR ELDERS"

Voices of wisdom, wise direction, self-correction

Encouraging us youngins to use introspection before correction

Our Elders are the winds of life that blows reminders of respect and dignity to all mankind regardless, of age, race, or creed

Indeed, our Elders are the most precious beautiful giants in our lives, full of wisdom, experience and lessons.

Your mark on life is made with every child you've had to raise

With every prayer you prayed

With your hands to God in praise

With your voice used to lift his name

Your mark on life is made.

Making your community a better place, with the sweat equity and labor you gave

Training up next generations to love each other

Speak to one another
Abort and avoid foolish pride
And take it one day at a time.

Don't take cuts, stand in line and wait your turn
What you want in life, you must earn
Feverishly teaching us about what it means to have respect demand respect and dignity
Embedding these truths as a non-negotiable to our life's fabric
In order that we may avoid colliding into self-destructive habits.

We praise your dedication and teaching with much adoration
We give reverence to you today, because the beauty and enlightenment that you, as our Elders, have paved the way
for us to see, foresee and believe that it is our responsibility to leave a mark in life as you've so freely given and we've so freely received.

As we praise God for our beautiful Elders, we are reminded of His word and instructions
Proverbs 23:22, "Listen to your father, who gave you life and do not despise your mother when she is old."

Exodus 20:12- "Honor your father and mother, that your days may be long in the land which the Lord your God give you."

We are appreciative of your humor and wit
Teaching us about lessons on living
We are most grateful for the precious moments and memories we have with you.

Your spiritual and relentless guidance is the beauty that God has kissed us with for a lifetime.

-This is dedicated to Lorraine, Beverly, Kori, Phyllis, Marvie, Tanisa, Keisha E., LaCrecia C., Wanda, Edrina, Shani and Lakeisha-

"THE BEAUTY OF MY SISTERS"

To my rough riders

Strength resides insides us

Potential can't hide from us.

Ups and downs

Life's turn-a-rounds

But, that's besides us

God has our backs and he's right beside us.

He knows what's best for us

No need to guess, for what's next

He keeps up with us

So in him we must trust

Not our luck

Or our fate
But our faith, we must trust.

Many nights we've wrestled with what's next?
What's best?
What's left?
What should we expect?

But, we kept the fight
We made it through the night
God promises proved that we'd be alright.

Tears that flow
Only God really knows
But a sister can feel, when near
Feel when you're hurting
When there's fear.

Dear Sisters:
I love you and I will be here for you. I've got your back and I'm praying for you. So let us remain steadfast and unmovable, because God's deliverance is "provable". Look at how he has held you, kept you and never once let you go. God hears my

prayers for you and I trust he knows just what to do. So, have the assurance that his grace is sufficient to see you through from your story to your glory.

-Dedicated To Every Beautiful Woman-

"There's Something Wrong with Your Love Story"

A few minutes of touching and hugging and you're calling it love? It's something wrong with your love story, Baby.

Pretty is what's inside

Pretty is where the soul resides

Pretty doesn't compromise

Pretty doesn't accept the bitter sweet tainted lies.

It's not too late to rewrite your love story.

You're pretty because you value your temple

You're pretty because something inside speaks, your eyes wink, and your heart beats because you understand the rhythm in your feet

And you walk to a new sound

Finding the solid rock

Standing on the rock
Avoiding the pitfalls on shaky grounds
You will not be defeated by the appetizers that the devil tries to convince you to eat.

See, there's something wrong with your love story, if God doesn't get the glory.

Your heart should be smitten, hidden in God that "he" has to seek God just to find you
Does this describe your Beau?

If what I'm giving sound true
Then it's up to you to rename your love story
Change the characters
Find a new hook
Change the title
Open the cover and read
I am who God says I am
I am precious to God
I'm the King's daughter
I am a part of a Royal Priesthood and a Holy Nation.

I'm Pretty because I'm reminded of the truth.

-Inspired by Mary Henderson-
(Colorist/Stylist @Meagan Mitchell Salon)

"Mary, Mary, the Hair Fairy"

Hey Baby Girl, Lil Momma
You always find a woman that wherever she goes
Her maternal instinct flows.

Her concern reaches to raise a nation of women because she identifies what's in them
She sees their experiences through the windows of the past using her earlier lenses to share her wisdom.

She hears their stories and tells them the truth about what's in them
Transparency she uses to build a legacy to help with the understanding and building of their identity.

A bigger than life character she is

With a joyful smile, jazz in her step, style in her hips,
And color in her hair.

But don't be fooled by her light-hearted spirit and her sound of laughter
Cause' her stories don't lie and her truths are put to life's pages help set the stage for a better performance that one day we might play.

So, the spirit of our grands and great-grands take an encore when life lessons flow from her
Whether it's a dance, one word or a story heard
Listen
Learn
Perform.

-Inspired by Dr. Rebecca James Williams-

"THE BEAUTY OF LISTENING"

Listen to your body when it clicks, tic-tock, tic-tock

Listen to your body when it tells you to quit- smokin, druggin, usin, abusin.

Listen to your body when it speaks.
But do we listen?

It cries
Do we care?
It laughs
Do we enjoy?
It struggles
But do we share?
It screams
Do we know how to turn the volume down?

Or do we just depend on others to interpret, instruct and diagnose?

Listen first
It speaks to us
Listen
Stop
Slow down
Listen and respond with
healthier choices
It belongs to God,
So cherish, respect and value it by
Listening.

-Dedicated to Ms. Patty-

"A REMODELED ANGEL"

Wide brim hats

Louis Vutton luggage and handbags

Blinged out caps

No talking crap to Ms. Patty

And she takes no lip lashing.

Mysterious and unique

A front row seat for Ms. Patty

There is nothing second class about this woman.

A quiet strength is noticed

Her influence run deep, from the Eastside to the Westside

And from the East Coast to the West Coast

Ms. Patti's village runs deep.

No one is ever tossed away

No one is ever too far away

Ms. Patty helps the entire village and is there to stay.

When you see her raising her hands on Sundays
Waving her word on Wednesdays
Bringing the village to God, occupying the entire pew
Understand and know that this the manifestation of God's remodeled Angel.

Ms. Patty, let your light shine so that others may see that God can do all things, anything and everything when you let him in.

-Inspired by the Documentary Love is Not a Black Eye-

"LOVE IS NOT A BLACK EYE"

He hits, she falls

She screams- he calls

Her names that her mother didn't give her

She crawls from low self-esteem to what do you mean I'm a-

Which day is it, because I've been hit, again

By my, boyfriend?

But this time with words that he used to destroy me

With secrets shared and insight that even I didn't see

But because I told him all about me

He turned around and used it on me

But I believed what he said

Cause, it showed that he cared.

He was concern enough to scream, sometimes

Doesn't that mean he cares, sometimes?
He showed me some attention and affection
Never wanting to be alone or feel rejection.

He held me close with his choke hold
I thought it was an emotional expression of affection
But then he pushed me off with words of rejection.

"Ain't nobody gonna ever want you, but me!"
I stood frozen and still just like a watercolor portrait of a painted tree.

So, here come the tears strolling down memory lane
Why does this feel the same?
Why am I insane to think that things will change?
If I remain, believing and feeding these sick demon of lies, with muffled cries in my room at night so that my children don't see me bleed.

The cut across my face, the bruise on my heart and the irreversible thought I sought after to prove is true
If you love me, you should hit me with your words of destruction

And your words that break me down and make me feel like love has been abducted from me

Hiding from me, blinding me from seeing

Seeing,

Singing,

Living,

Feeling,

But, yet keeps me spinning

I'm still not winning.

But, there I stand in the middle of a mirror trying to cover up bruises from the pain

Fighting to stay sane

Until one day, I told myself, I tried to believe myself, but then I asked myself

"Love is not a black eye?"

Will somebody answer me please!

Soul Sista #Won

"THE BEAUTY OF MY SISTAS"

Soul Sista

Bold Sista

You are gold, Sista

You can't fold Sista

You are precious in your

Platforms

Afros

Stilettos

Locks

Press and Curls

Kiss Curls

Perms

Weaves

Bangle Bracelets

True Religion Jeans

Prada Shoes

Louis Vuitton

Mac Makeup

David Yurmon

and

St. John Suits

Speak wise words that falls from the experiences of wisdom with a poetic potion that feed and fuel the souls of your younger daughters, sisters and your mothers.

Go ahead and dance like you know God is going to trouble the waters, while keeping your eyes on God.

Sing with victory whaling from the bottom of your belly swelling the world with your awesome cries of how you overcame it and now they know you as an Overcomer.

Laugh until tears crawl down your face formulate a puddle of old memories that you now stand in as a reflection of lessons earned and learned.

You've Won the battles of womanhood
You've Won the battles of motherhood
You've Won the battles of being misunderstood
You've Won many battles.

So, go ahead Soul Sista
Stand bold, Sista
Cause you didn't fold, Sista

You're precious like gold, Sista

Have you yet been told, Sista

Then, you're owed, Sista

To know that you are fearfully and wonderfully made

And when God made you he didn't make no mistakes

He made a ministry

So go run and tell it, Sista!

Dorothea Sharon

About the Author

Dorothea Sharon, a respected and sought after producer, director, playwright, performance poet and actress. Her mission in life is to educate people using innovative and creative methods. Dorothea is on track to change theater and stage production as we know it. She has toured nationally with many musical stage productions including Michael Matthew's *Wicked Ways*, David E. Talbert's *What Goes Around Comes Around*, Bennine Rodgers's *Only the Strong*, and Angel Barrow-Dunlap's *If These Hips Could Talk*.

Characterized by her electrifying energy on and off the stage, she has worked with incredible artists *including* Tishina Arnold, Darin Henson, Johnson Hinton, Carl Payne, Regina King, Lisa Raye, David Hollister, A.J. Johnson, Tony Roberts, the legendary Billy Dee Williams, and the gospel greats, Kim Burrell, Vanessa Bell Armstrong, Fred Hammond and Marvin Sapp.

With the zeal for cutting-edge theatrical innovation, Dorothea has received accolades, as the writer/producer and director of the dramatic stage musical, *Strong Women Keep Coming*. She has shared accolades as director and contributing writer for the hit touring stage musical, *If These Hips Could Talk*. Her works and credits have been acknowledged in publications such as *The Jet* and *Sister 2 Sister* magazines.

Dorothea is also a writer and artist who is committed to being a *change* agent in the lives of others through innovative and artistic platforms. She is one of the program directors for D.R.E.A.M. Girls mentoring program at Second Ebenezer Church. Dorothea is also a founding member of The G.A.L. Collective, a guild of female artists who are committed to lending significant time, talent and their expertise to support women and at-risk girls.

She holds a Master of Science in Counseling/Mental Health Counseling and a Master of Arts in Education/Adult Education and Training from University of Phoenix. She graduated from Central Michigan University where she earned her undergraduate degree in Applied Arts and Science/Broadcasting and Cinematic Arts. Her sights are set on utilizing all of her creative talents to create programs, platforms and performances that ignite growth and development for the human spirit.

Her most recent work was released in November, 2011, *Love is Not a Black Eye*, a documentary about domestic violence. Dorothea is currently working on her second documentary, *There's Something Wrong with Your Love Story*.

www.ingramcontent.com/pod-product-compliance
Lightning Source LLC
Chambersburg PA
CBHW071131090426
42736CB00012B/2094